SUCCESS

Sprouting is the easiest way to provide yourself with a constant supply of fresh, nutritious vegetable food with a minimum of time and effort. This book explains the whole process and includes a large number of delicious sprout recipes.

SUCCESSFUL SPROUTING

Fresh Nutrition-packed Food from Your Window Ledge

by

FRANK WILSON

Illustrations by Ray Barnett

NATURE'S WAY

THORSONS PUBLISHERS LIMITED
Wellingborough, Northamptonshire

First published 1978
Second Impression 1979
Third Impression 1980

ISBN 0 7225 0440 3

.Photoset in Great Britain by
Specialised Offset Services Ltd, Liverpool
and printed by
Weatherby Woolnough Ltd,
Wellingborough, Northants.

CONTENTS

CHAPTER ONE

Sprouting – An Approach to Health

Both consumers and suppliers of health foods, if their approach is genuine, are on the look-out for foods which contain as many of the natural vitamins, minerals and other nutritional substances as possible, are produced in as natural a way as possible, and undergo an absolute minimum of the processing which usually tends to detract from the basic nutritional value. Nature in her wisdom has provided a fine balance of vital nutritional substances in our food and it is all too easy to upset and destroy them.

In the hurly-burly of modern living we rely on a complicated food chain for the supply of our food and this in turn means that the longer the chain, the greater becomes the need for preservatives and ensuring the food is capable of maintaining a long shelf life.

For example, a particular commodity may well have to endure transportation in adverse conditions in the country of origin, then be warehoused at the port of departure whilst awaiting a ship, survive several weeks in a cargo hold, and then further storage at the point of importation. After this it has to be moved to a distribution warehouse, as it is not practical to collect individual items from the dockside, and then goes either to a retail warehouse or direct to the retail shop. Then you have to allow a time in the shop as a sales period and a time in the housewife's larder before final consumption. There are many permutations of this problem depending on whether the food has to undergo any form of manufacturing process or not, and whether the product is of seasonal growth but is required by the consumer throughout the year.

The pace of modern day life has encouraged manufacturers to produce more and more convenience foods ready packaged, quickly prepared, frequently highly coloured and flavoured, and certainly with the actual nutritional value coming as a last and very unimportant consideration.

In such foods, packaging is usually extremely attractive and readily catches the eye of the shopper. Indeed, not infrequently, the cost of the packaging is higher than the cost of the food itself.

ADVANTAGES OF BUYING SEEDS FOR SPROUTING

From this it will be seen that a lightweight, easily carried packet of seeds which, with a very little careful planning and with even less effort, can be purchased, taken home and sprouted, must be an attractive proposition to any shopper, young or old, who is genuinely interested in a convenience food which is not only convenient, but highly nutritious as well.

Basically, then, the value of sprouts is threefold: the seeds themselves are easily transported from the shop to the home; the preparation required to turn the seeds into sprouts is absolutely minimal; the sprouts themselves provide fresh shoots which are extremely rich in vitamin C and frequently in carotene and B Complex, together with other vitamins according to the nature of the seeds themselves, and all with valuable trace elements and minerals. As has already been said, they are easily purchased, easily prepared and when consumed they are very speedily and easily assimilated to provide the vitamin and mineral needs of our bodies.

Sprouts prepared at home in this way are eaten as required and do not have a chance to lose their nutritional value – you just grow them on a scale and at a rate to suit your own personal needs.

CHAPTER TWO

The History of Sprouting

From the beginning of time, Man has worshipped the 'life force' in one form or another. To do so is, of course, natural as without it he would not exist. He realizes this and it is therefore sacred to him.

Man has worshipped the sun and the rain and he has prayed to his gods for good harvests; for his desires to come to fruition; for the 'horn of plenty'. It is only in birth and the creation of new life and new things that Man can perpetuate his existence and justify his place on this earth. The fact that not too infrequently his creations turn sour on him and the whole purpose of existence is brought into question does not alter the fact that without the 'life force' and the total philosophy of that force, Man himself would not be here.

It is therefore easy to understand the importance that was placed on the production of new life during the history of Man, and this applied to vegetable as well as animal, including the human animal. As Man evolved, the wonder of this life force came to be appreciated by him, and as he did not understand it, it became a thing to be marvelled at, and indeed to be worshipped. Hence in the history of the various countries of the world where earlier civilizations existed we see the gradual evolution of drawings and paintings illustrating this wonder and we see the selection of certain species for worship as 'sacred'. One such example was the Quinoa plant grown in Central America and believed to have been regarded as sacred by the Incas.

THE FIRST RECOGNITION
Having these thoughts in mind, it is not difficult to understand the fascination which a new plant shoot could produce for Man. Here was a hard little seed, generally brown or grey in colour, sometimes wrinkled, and all too frequently indistinguishable from its surrounding gravel or sand, that suddenly with a drop of rain, a little warmth from the sun, split open and in no time at all started to produce the first green shoots of an entirely new plant.

Man soon recognized the life force

involved and appreciated that here it was in its very essence and at its most vital moment. Maybe he did not understand metabolism or the importance of vitamins and minerals, but he could recognize that, at this moment when the shoot started to grow, he had the essence of life before him.

SPROUTING IN CHINA

Not unnaturally in view of their sophisticated civilization at a time when, in Western Europe, we were still living in caves, the Chinese reasoned that to use such new shoots for foods would provide a simple yet highly effective addition to diet. So it appears that as long ago as 3000 B.C. the use of bean shoots had begun in China and has continued ever since.

There are suggestions that the Aztecs, too, indulged in this form of food, but records of the civilization of the Aztecs are not as clear as those of the Chinese. Certainly, the Navajo Indians were aware of the use of sprouts and it is certainly reasonable to suppose that the Chinese did not have exclusive rights in the ancient world to this type of reasoning or to its practice.

One could also speculate on the use of sprouting procedures by ancient civilizations on long sea voyages, and although even as recently as the early part of the twentieth century there was still talk of scurvy, perhaps the Phoenicians had, in their day, overcome this problem. However, this is pure supposition, albeit a fascinating idea, and it is China that we accept as being the originator of this type of food.

THE SITUATION TODAY

In 3000 B.C. bean sprouts were an important nutrient in China and today they are still important, not only for use in China itself, but for canning and exporting to the Western world. This exportation of canned shoots to the Western world began in the first place as a novelty, something a little different to add variety to the dinner party, and to a certain extent this attitude still prevails. However, in recent years the true value of sprouts has begun to be appreciated in the West, not only for the highly palatable nature of the sprout itself, but from the point of view of the nutritional aspect, and it is the latter which is today beginning to assume importance. To get the full benefit of the nutrients, the seeds should be freshly sprouted, following the procedures described later in this book, so that they are eaten at the very moment when they are at the peak of their nutritional value.

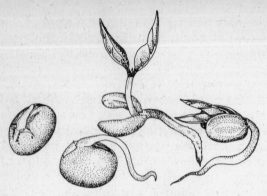

CHAPTER THREE

Seed Formation and Development

When the parent plant first sheds its seed, the seed enters into a resting period. During this time there is little apparent change and it respires at a very low rate. However, during this time, the capacity of the seed to germinate does change and this ripening period varies very considerably, both with the species of plant from which the seed has come and with the climatic or storage conditions. Even when seeds have in fact developed to a state of potential germination they may, again according to species, persist in this condition for a very long time, sometimes years. Generally, seeds retain their germinating viability longest in cold, dry conditions.

Seeds have a basic structure, which consists of an embryo which will produce the new plant, the endosperm which is the food store on which the embryo will have to live when it first becomes active, and the cotyledons which either store additional nourishments or act as agents in the transfer of nutritional matter from the endosperm (store) to the new plant. The seed itself is then surrounded by a series of hard, protective fibrous layers to insulate it against the external conditions of rain, snow, frost and excessive sun. Within the seed, the embryo, which will produce the new plant, has two growing points: the radicle which produces the new shoot and the tenule which produces the root.

WATER CONTENT

The change from dormant seed into active sprouts is largely dominated by the supply of water. The most striking aspect of the physical state of the resting seed is the extremely low water content. Normally actively metabolizing tissue contains about 90 per cent water, whereas the resting seed has only about 10 per cent. No rapid germination can begin until the water level rises dramatically, and this absorption of water into the germinating seed takes place in two stages.

In the first stage water is drawn into the seed and is distributed over the internal surfaces. This initial intake of water is quite substantial, but will be retarded in the case of hard seeds because the water will have difficulty in penetrating the outer seed coat. The process can be accelerated if the outer seed coat is broken. During this initial intake of water the seed swells, but this must not be taken as a sign of growth; that only comes in the second stage. The second stage still requires a good supply of water but this has to be combined with the right temperature if growth and development are to occur. Naturally, the optimum temperature will vary with the species involved. Seeds of species from temperate climates usually do well at about 68°F (20°C), whereas the tropical species need a temperature of, say, 86-95°F (30-35°C).

During the second stage the individual cells of the embryo grow in a process of rapid metabolism which initially provides cell extension and then causes the cells to divide. Water and oxygen are essential and the embryo plant contains vital amino acids and minerals from the endosperm. When the embryo has developed into a seedling, and when the embryonic roots, leaves and stem have been transformed into mature organs, germination is complete and the seedling becomes independent of food reserves in the endosperm, which it had to rely on in the early stages.

WHY SPROUTS RATHER THAN SEEDS?

The seed, before sprouting begins, is a valuable source of protein as well as being rich in carbohydrates and having some vitamins and minerals. But most seeds are not particularly digestible and many people avoid them for this reason. The sprouted seed, however, becomes less fattening as much of the carbohydrate store has been used up, and becomes more digestible as the fats and starches are changed into vitamins, sugars, minerals, and proteins. So, in addition to digestibility, this is certainly good news for weight watchers.

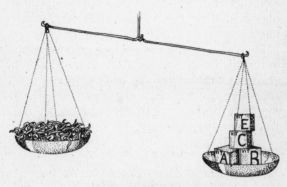

CHAPTER FOUR

Sprouts and Their Nutritional Value

It was indicated in the previous chapter that as seeds germinated and began to sprout they increased their vitamin and mineral value. Both vitamins and minerals are absolutely vital to bodily health and even in highly sophisticated societies it is by no means unusual to find people with certain deficiencies in these two vital areas. It is only in the twentieth century that we have begun to realize the importance of vitamins and minerals in our diet. As food production increases, and in the course of so doing becomes more sophisticated, so there has been an increasing trend towards foods which have either become denatured in the course of the processes which they have passed through, or lost much of their natural value and have then had a part of this value synthetically put back.

The main vitamin losses are undoubtedly in the water soluble vitamins, particularly B complex and vitamin C, but other vitamins are also drastically affected by many modern methods of production, as are the all-important minerals.

VITAMIN CONTENT

To return to the subject of sprouting, however, the scientific evaluation of the changes which take place when seed starts to sprout is still very much in its infancy and it may be some time before a truly comprehensive picture is available. Much of the research in these changes has, and is, being carried out in the United States of America, where increases of over 300 per cent in vitamin A value and up to as much as 600 per cent in vitamin C value have been registered in certain seeds when they have been sprouted. In many instances, according to the type of sprout, there have also been very substantial increases in the range of B group vitamins and in vitamin E.

MINERAL CONTENT

The mineral content, which is so often overlooked because of the emphasis which is given to vitamins, but which is in fact so very important to the maintenance of good bodily health, has been chelated in the sprouts and is ready for immediate use by the body. Conversion of the seed from starches to simple sugars therefore means that the energy which they supply and the extremely high vitamin and mineral content which develops can quickly and easily be assimilated by the human body. In order that we may fully understand the need for vitamins in our diet, a vitamin table is given on page 20.

As a further guide to the value of individual sprouts there is also a table of a number of popular sprouts with the vitamins which are predominantly present when sprouting takes place (see page 21).

As well as the nutritional advantages, which are many, and the simplicity of this food source, there is of course the sheer fun of growing your own vegetables as you want them, when you want them, and where you want them, without even having to go and dig the garden. It is perhaps the lazy gardener's answer to fresh food production with a minimum amount of work, and with the knowledge that you could hardly better the end product in nutritional value.

Vitamin and Mineral Table	
The Vitamins	*Their Use*
A	Essential for reducing the risk of infection, keeping skin healthy and protecting against eye-strain.
B	The B complex controls the metabolism of fats, proteins and carbohydrates. No diet is complete unless it contains the B vitamins in adequate amounts.
C	Increases resistance to infection, and aids recovery after illness. Assists utilization of other vitamins and minerals.
D	Helps the body to absorb calcium and phosphorus. Assists formation of bones and strong teeth.
E	Deficiency causes poor circulation (pins and needles, cold extremities, chilblains, cramp), hardened arteries, thrombosis, phlebitis, varicose veins.
The Minerals	
Calcium and Phosphorus	In adults, during pregnancy and old age, for vegans and in all cases of calcium deficiency and for protecting teeth and bones. In children for building strong bones, nails and sound teeth. Promotes growth.
Iron	Common symptoms of iron deficiency are fatigue, rough skin and brittle hair, susceptibility to infections, palpitations, loss of appetite, breathlessness.
Iodine	Promotes physical and mental energy and alertness. Aids assimilation of Vitamin E.

Vitamin Content of Sprouts	
Adzuki Beans	Vitamin B1, B2, Iron, Potassium
Alfalfa	Vitamin D, E, K and C, Iron, Phosphorus
Barley	Vitamin B1, B2, C
Blackeye Beans	Vitamin B1, C, Iron, Niacin
Chick Peas	Vitamin C, B1, Iron
Fenugreek	Vitamin A, C, Iron
Lentils	Vitamin B1, B2, C, Iron
Lima Beans	Vitamin B1, B2, C, Iron, Niacin
Millet	Vitamin B1, B2, C
Mung Beans	Vitamin A, C, E, Choline
Oats	Vitamin B1, B2, C, Iron
Radish	Vitamin A, B1, C, Iron, Phosphorus
Red Wonder Beans	Vitamin B1, B2, Iron, Niacin, Phosphorus, Potassium
Rice	Vitamin B1, B2, C, Iron
Soya Beans	Vitamin B, E
Sunflower	Vitamin C, E

CHAPTER FIVE

Methods of Sprouting

There are many methods of sprouting, some complex with sophisticated equipment, others simple with virtually no equipment at all. It is possible to buy a tiered plastic sprouter, for example, which will enable you to grow a number of sprouts of different varieties in the same vessel at the same time. However, sprouting is a very elementary and natural thing and perhaps it is not unreasonable to express some preference for a more basic method.

Whichever method you use, it is important to select your seeds with discrimination and it pays dividends to pick them over carefully and to discard those which are cracked or old-looking.

THE BASIC METHOD
One of the most satisfactory basic methods

of sprouting requires only a glass jar, a piece of muslin and an elastic band. Having picked over the beans carefully, place them in water to soak overnight. During this initial soaking period the beans will increase to about double their original size as they absorb water in the first stage of sprouting. Next, drain off the beans, wash them in fresh cool water and drain off the rinsing water. Do not leave any water in the container at this stage. The jar should then be laid on its side in a position that is out of direct sunlight and where there is good ventilation. Remember, the three prime requirements for successful sprouting are water, good ventilation and warmth. Some 'sprouters' advocate darkness but from my own experience this is generally disadvantageous and tends to inhibit more rapid sprouting and the natural formation of chlorophyll in the sprout itself.

Every morning and evening, the muslin should be removed, the seeds rinsed in water, the muslin replaced and the water drained off through the muslin.

STORAGE OF SPROUTS

In most cases the seeds will start to sprout on the second day, and most will grow at a rapid rate. If you find that you have more than you require, you may either refrigerate them in a covered container or oven-dry them and store in a cool dry place. You do, of course, lose some nutritional value in this process. Having oven-dried them you have a choice of either storing them as they are, or grinding them first, so that if you do grow sprouts in excess of your immediate requirements, they certainly need not be wasted. If you wish to grow larger amounts of sprouts, you can use a large plastic container, but it is important to ensure that with a larger container they still get sufficient fresh air as they will otherwise tend to ferment and become rancid.

An alternative method for sprouting is to use an unglazed dish: having soaked the seeds in the normal way, place them in the dish and stand the dish in water.

A way of producing larger quantities of seed is to make a sprouting tray, which is merely a large tray containing muslin or tissues on which the seeds are placed after their initial soaking. The sprouting trays lose their moisture much more quickly through evaporation than the jam jar, and therefore require a little more attention and more frequent applications of water so that the seeds are kept moist. The more sophisticated methods using specially designed equipment invariably have operating instructions peculiar to the equipment in question, but all work on the same basic principle.

ADDITIONAL EQUIPMENT
If you wish to buy equipment, the most satisfactory type is the sprouting tube. For regular 'sprouters' this is undoubtedly the ideal method and the initial outlay is soon repaid in production. The sprouting tube is a jar which is open at each end and has caps of varying type and mesh which can

be placed on the end according to the size of the seed being sprouted. With this method you can quite quickly obtain a 'block of sprouts' and with the variable mesh you have the option of draining off the water or actually shaking out the bean or seed husks. Incidentally, these husks do give added roughage if you leave them. Special plastic sprouting tubes are produced but again you can improvise. All you really need is a plastic tube made of good quality clear plastic. It should be 9-12 inches (22-30cm) in length and about 3 inches (7.5cm) in diameter. Instead of caps at each end you can use muslin or similar material held in place with elastic bands as in the jam jar method.

CHAPTER SIX

The Range of Sprouting Beans and Seeds

One should eat sprouts when they are young; the majority are at their tastiest when between $\frac{3}{8}$ and $\frac{3}{4}$ inch (9 and 19mm) in length. You will soon be able to gauge your daily requirements and sprout accordingly to avoid excess production and consequent wastage.

When selecting your seeds, you should make a point of choosing ones which have not been chemically treated. Health food stores are of course a natural source of chemically untreated foods, and seeds and beans bought from them are generally most suitable for sprouting. After all, if you are going to use seeds which have been treated, this treatment will concentrate chemicals into the new plant life.

The main chemicals to be found in treated seeds are pesticides, and the basic philosophy of health foods must be to avoid such chemicals. In addition to ordinary pesticides, the seeds are sometimes treated with fungicides and mould inhibitors, as well as occasionally with dyes for identification purposes. So make sure that you get untreated seeds.

It is best to look for seeds that have been selected primarily for sprouting, quite apart from the aspect of treatment, as these will be in a prime condition; not cracked, broken or past the age when successful sprouting will occur. To a large extent one has to rely on the supplier, so make sure that you go to a reputable store.

Some people grow their own seed for sprouting and to do this adds still further to the interest and fascination of this type of food production. Again, ensure that the plants themselves are free from chemicals and only pick the seeds when they have reached maturity. They should be put in a cool, dark place, which must also be completely dry, and must then be left there to dry out.

TYPES OF SEED

Here then is a list of a number of seeds which may be used: it is by no means complete, but will provide a general guide.

Adzuki Bean. This is a smallish red bean which developed in China and Japan and only more recently became popular in the Western world. It has a fairly mild, although distinctive, bean flavour and is fairly easy to sprout, with a sprouting time of four to six days. The sprouts should be allowed to develop to about $\frac{3}{4}$ inch (18mm) and may be used in salads, side dishes or as a buttered main dish.

Alfalfa. This seed is very easy to sprout. If used at about $\frac{1}{4}$ inch (6mm) it may be oven-dried, browned and either mixed with cereals or put in bread. Alternatively, it may be allowed to develop up to $1\frac{1}{2}$ inches (3.5cm) and used as an addition to salad or as a side dish. It takes five or six days to reach 1 inch (2.5cm) in length.

Barley. Another crop from ancient times, the seed was known in China and in Egypt from at least 2000 B.C. It is also produced in Europe, China, the United States, parts of India, North Africa, and the Balkans. Barley has a number of culinary uses and, like rice, has a medicinal value. There is a problem in obtaining untreated seeds for sprouting, but if you are able to get them, the sprouting time is three to five days. The sprouts are rather more bitter in flavour than oats, but they are used in much the same way.

Black Beans. These are a product of the American continent. The sprouts should be allowed to develop to about $\frac{1}{2}$ inch (1.25cm) which will take three to five days. It is useful in side dishes or as an additional flavour for salads.

Blackeye Beans. These beans are a good source of protein with similar sprouting characteristics and uses as black beans.

Buckwheat. Originating in the East, buckwheat was taken across Europe in the Middle Ages and later to America by the settlers. Buckwheat is a very fast growing grain with a sprouting time of two to four days. The sprouts may be used in lengths varying from $\frac{1}{4}$ inch (6mm) to 1 inch (2.5cm), according to taste. The flavour is distinctive and the sprouts make good main dishes as well as being tasty additions in soups and salads. They can also be oven-dried and ground for mixing in bread.

Chia. This comes from Mexico, and again is not generally available in Europe. It has a distinctive strong flavour, which has to be acquired, and a rapid sprouting time of two days.

Chick Peas. The chick pea, also known as the garbanzo bean, is grown in parts of Europe and in North America. It is a good source of protein but the beans themselves should be checked carefully for damage before being used for sprouting. They should be allowed to develop to about 1 inch (2.5cm), which will take five to eight days. Like soya beans, they will tend to spoil if allowed to remain too wet for too long. Their main use is in salads, side dishes or as a cooked vegetable.

Cress. This is a fast grower with a sprout that reaches about 1 inch (2.5cm) after four days. It has a distinctive taste and is used on salads and in sandwiches.

Fenugreek. This is becoming increasingly well known in the Western world, although it originated in the East, where it is used for seasoning. The sprouting time is two to four days and sprouts should not be allowed to develop much beyond a quarter of an inch (6mm) as they then lose their spicy flavour and tend to become bitter. Fenugreek is ideal in salads or side dishes.

Lentils. These sprout in three to four days, and should be allowed to grow to approximately $\frac{1}{2}$ inch (12mm). They are a very valuable source of high protein, and come in various strains which can either be reddish to brown, or grey-green in colour, according to variety. They have a very distinctive bean flavour and make a pleasant and nutritious addition to salads, side dishes, and so on. They can be oven-dried and used to add flavour to a number of recipes.

Lima Beans. This large white bean has a good flavour providing the sprout does not develop more than $\frac{1}{2}$ inch (12mm). Sprouting time is about six days, and the beans are generally used as an addition to salads. It is very important not to oversoak the bean in its early stages as this will cause it to ferment.

Maize. This seed is probably one of the oldest-known seeds in the world, its history stretching back into biblical times when the Israelites migrated to Egypt. It has always been a popular seed because of its very high yield and robust characteristics. It is found in the United States, South America, Europe, Canada, South Africa, India and Australia, but is relatively difficult to obtain in an untreated state. The sprouting time is generally three to six days and the sprouts can be used in salads, served separately with butter or added to soups and other dishes.

Millet. Millet originated in Africa and Asia. Its sprouting time is three to five days, and it can be used buttered as a main dish, or as a side dish as well as in cereals. The sprouts can also be dried in an oven and used in bread.

Mung Bean. This tiny green bean is the original Chinese sprouting bean. Easy to grow, it has a delicious fresh bean flavour; it needs relatively little attention and is a good source of protein. Sprouting time varies with temperature but it generally takes three to five days and sprouts are ideal at about $\frac{1}{2}$ inch (12mm) in length, although some people prefer the slightly stronger flavour which develops with longer sprouts. Mung beans are delicious in salads, side dishes or as main dishes, and can also be oven dried and used either whole or ground.

Oats. Oats are a product of North America, northern areas of Europe and parts of Russia. The sprouting time for oats is three to five days and they have a pleasant flavour mixed with salads or buttered and served separately. They require less water than most seeds and the pre-soaking period should be restricted to between thirty and sixty minutes. Only use oats which still have the outer hull intact.

Pumpkin. It is not always easy to get unhulled pumpkin seeds which are very necessary for successful sprouting. However, they are well worth the effort as they are highly nutritious. The sprouts should be used before they reach $\frac{1}{2}$ inch (12mm) in length and the sprouting time is two to five days.

Quinoa. Developed in the high Andes and regarded as sacred by the Incas, these seeds are generally unavailable outside the American continent. They are an important crop for a number of South American countries and have sprouting characteristics similar to maize.

Radish. The seeds are either red or black, and for sprouting purposes there is little difference. The main advantage of a radish sprout is that it gives a tangy, peppery taste and can therefore be used to garnish other dishes.

Red Wonder Beans. Known both in Europe and America, this bean will provide a useful addition to salads. It has a sprouting time of three to six days.

Rice. This is grown widely in the Far East, and in the United States, France and Italy, and is one of the world's main staple foods. It has a high nutritional value and also a medicinal use for soothing certain digestive troubles. It is very good for sprouting and the grain is of course easy to obtain. For successful sprouting, which takes three to five days, you require unpolished rice – brown rice without the outer protective covering taken away. Again, unpolished rice is invariably available at health food stores, and can be obtained in two varieties – the long grain or the round grain. Both are nutritionally similar and both sprout equally well. Rice sprouts are usually rather more bland in flavour than others, sprout easily and are excellent in salads, soups or as an additional vegetable for use with main dishes.

Rye. This crop is grown in North America and Europe, and the sprouts can be used in salads, soups and side dishes. The sprouting time is three to five days and for soups they should be allowed to grow to no more than $\frac{1}{2}$ inch (12mm), whereas for salads they may be grown to $1\frac{1}{2}$ inches (3.5cm) without losing tenderness.

Soya Bean. Soya is well known for its food value, as it is the only first-class protein which is entirely vegetable. It was originally grown in China, then spread to other parts of the Far East, and more recently was developed in the United States and Canada. Today it is widely used in the form of soya flour, or for bean soup, or as text-ured protein for meat substitutes. The sproutings of soya beans may be used in salads or with side dishes, or covered with butter as a main dish. They may also be oven-dried, ground and added to bread or other dishes.

The taste of the sprouts is on the strong side and for this reason it is important not to allow them to develop beyond $\frac{3}{4}$ inch

(18mm) if you wish to eat them raw.
Indeed, many people like to steam this
bean before using it in uncooked dishes.
However, if you wish to use them as a
cooked vegetable you can allow them to
grow to $1\frac{1}{4}$ (3cm) inches. The sprouting
time is three to seven days and whilst they
require a certain amount of water they
must not be allowed to stay too wet for too
long as they have a tendency to ferment.
Soya beans are sometimes damaged in
transit and may well split and go mouldy. It
is important, therefore, to select your
beans carefully for sprouting purposes.

Sunflower. The sunflower is a particularly
valuable plant as, in addition to its diuretic
medicinal use, its seeds are a source of oils
in the polyunsaturate range. There are two
basic varieties, the black sunflower seed
and the white sunflower seed (although
the latter sometimes has black longitudinal
stripes). The seeds have a pleasant nutty
flavour and a high nutritional value, and it
is for this reason that the majority of health
food stores stock and sell considerable
quantities.

The oil from the sunflower seed provides
the polyunsaturate oil which those
concerned with food reform and
cholesterol levels regard as being so
important. They are also a valuable mineral
source and this is why the seeds themselves
are very popular both as a sprouting plant
and for eating whole and being sprinkled
on salads.

Some care has to be taken when

sprouting sunflower seeds as the sprouting time is longer – generally five to eight days – and the sprouts must be eaten when they grow to $\frac{1}{4}$ inch (6mm) at the most, as they develop a strong, bitter flavour beyond this point. Sunflower sprouts are mainly used in salads but can be added to soups. You need the unhulled seed for successful sprouting.

Triticale. This is a fairly modern development of robust and fast-growing seed, which is a cross between rye and wheat. The sprouting time is rapid, one to three days, and its uses are similar to that of maize. Triticale is particularly rich in amino acids.

Wheat. Again, this crop is grown all over the world, but particularly in north-west Europe, the United States, Canada, the Ukraine, Argentine, and north-west China, as well as in parts of Australia and India. It is, like maize, a very prolific grower, and very easy to sprout. Sprouting time is four to six days and the sprouts themselves may be used in the same way as maize.

Wild Rice. This product of North America may be used in a similar way to ordinary unpolished rice but has a rather shorter sprouting time.

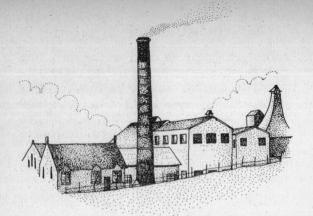

CHAPTER SEVEN

Commercial Applications of Sprouting

The main commercial application for sprouting is in the preparation of malt. Again, this is nothing new. Reference to Egyptian and Greek history suggests that even in those days fermented drinks were possibly prepared from a form of barley malt. Barley is, of course, the favoured commercial cereal, for several reasons.

The first is that it has a good record of germination and germinates very evenly with a high capacity. This, whilst important for domestic sprouting, is essential when applied on an industrial scale. The next asset is its hardiness and its resistance to damage during processing. Again, this is particularly important when industrial techniques are being applied.

The embryo development of the barley grain itself is also important because the roots emerge at a very early stage which enables the grain to be regularly layered at a consistent level (technically called couching). In addition, the husk layers of the grain provide efficient filtration, which in turn means a quicker and more even sprouting time.

Commercial malting provides malt for the distilling companies producing whisky, to the breadmaking industry for malt-flavoured bread, to the pharmaceutical industry for added malt flavouring, and by-products to the farming industry.

The essence of malting on a commercial scale is highly technical and requires sophisticated engineering techniques. Basically, it involves the hastening of the natural growth-rate of the grain, and then stopping the growth when it reaches the required limit. The aim is to form a product which, when water is added under appropriate conditions, will provide an extract containing materials on which yeast is able to feed, thus giving rise to a fermentation process, and in the same process producing a quantity of alcohol. The whole of the malting process is very similar to the domestic techniques which we have described earlier in this book, except for the fact that it is on a far larger scale. In the first instance the barley is steeped in water which washes the grain free from any surplus dirt and then encourages germination. As in the domestic approach, it is essential to have: (1) adequate moisture (2) a suitable temperature (3) plenty of air.

On a commercial scale steeping continues for approximately seventy-two hours and during this time there will be periods when the grain is completely submerged, and times when it is allowed to drain to allow the barley to respire. As the moisture in the barley increases, so does the respiration rate, and it then becomes essential that a form of aeration is introduced. Many of the more modern plants also use a technique for carbon dioxide extraction. The malting unit of barley is called a quarter, which when applied to unmalted barley is 448 lb. A quarter of barley will require up to 250 gallons of water.

After the steeping phase, the barley enters the germination period. The object of this part of the process is to obtain the reserve food materials in the embryo itself and get them to develop into a state where they can readily be hydrolyzed. In unmalted raw barley the enzyme system is completely unable to hydrolyze the starch in the kernel and form a suitable extract. With germination, however, this changes and during 'mashing' the enzyme system can hydrolyze the starch rapidly into its various sugars such as maltose.

In the older type of malthouses germination takes place on the floor of the malting, and after steeping, the grain is conveyed to an area or floor on which it can be spread out in a rectangular heap called a 'couch', which is normally approximately twelve inches thick. It then takes approximately twenty-four hours for the first sign of the root breaking out of the base, and at this stage it is spread out over the whole of the floor area in order that a constant temperature of 60°F can be obtained. In practice, about eighty square feet of floor space is required for each quarter of malt.

The growing period depends very much on the type of barley being used and the type of malt being required, and can last for anything from six to thirteen days.

The final stage in the malting process is to arrest germination, and this is done by kilning where the malt is rapidly dried and the moisture content reduced from forty to three per cent.

Malt produced for the brewing industry will be of varying degrees of colour depending on whether pale, medium or dark ales are required. This is governed by the temperature at which roasting is carried out. For the distilling industry, two basic types of malt are required: a high diastatic malt which is required for grain distillery, and a peat-flavoured malt for pot-stills. This is produced by drying over a peat fire so that the damp grain absorbs the aroma of the peat. In more recent years, a number of different types of maltings have developed, each with its own particular feature, its own degree of technology and with its own cost advantages and disadvantages. The various types are: (1) Saladin box maltings (2) Wanderhaufen maltings (3) Frauenheim Tower maltings (4) Static maltings (5) Domalt (6) Pot maltings (7) Drum maltings.

Whatever the method and whatever the efficiency of the system being used, the basic aim is to sprout. Malting is a vast subject and I have only described it from the point of view of interest to show how closely a vast industry is related to the method that you may well employ at home using a window ledge and a jam jar.

To conclude this particular chapter, I should mention my indebtedness to Granary Developments for providing me with facilities to visit their maltings and who gave me a great deal of technical information.

CHAPTER EIGHT

Some Recipes for Sprouts

If you are to be a successful sprouter, you must approach this whole development with a genuine interest, a sincere belief in the value to your health of what you are doing, and a very real desire to expand your knowledge. You must also have that sense of 'fun' which is necessary for any new venture. Remember, here you have an opportunity of producing high-quality food in the simplest possible way, without expensive equipment, and without any hard work. You have an opportunity to experiment and learn, and improve your own dietary intake at the same time. Certainly, in time you will become quite fascinated and want to pass the information which you glean on to other people. As the saying goes, 'an apple a day keeps the doctor away' – perhaps in future it will be a handful of sprouts instead of an apple.

Sprouting, as well as being useful, can become a hobby. As with most hobbies, start off simply and gradually develop. Experiment with your own equipment and gradually extend it. The improvement on equipment and extension into new realms of production with further cereals is all part of the fun, so where do you go for your seeds and for any equipment which you may need? The majority of health food stores will be able to help you, although they may not carry a full range of the seeds which you want. If your local health food store is not able to help you, G.R. Lane Health Products Ltd of Sissons Road, Gloucester, or Thompson and Morgan, seed merchants, of Ipswich, will be able to advise you as to stockists.

RECIPES

The following is a selection of recipes to start you off on using sprouts. There are endless variations to these recipes and indeed you can extend them into many other areas of the culinary art.

You will see as you go through them that in almost every case the use of herb or sea salt is recommended. This is because of the additional mineral value which is available and the greater flavour advantage.

In a number of instances yeast extract is included in recipes, and virtually any good quality yeast extract is suitable for this purpose. There are, however, one or two which specially commend themselves, one of which uses sea salt, and one or two which contain vegetable juices, thus improving the quality of the product still further.

When it comes to the use of oil sunflower seed oil or corn oil are recommended because they are both polyunsaturates and so low cholesterol oils; high cholesterol oils can lead to a hardening of the arteries with resultant circulatory conditions.

It does not take long to judge your sprout requirements, nor to form a pattern of growing which will give you a constant variety and add genuine sparkle to your enjoyment of food. If at any time you find that you have an excess of sprouts to your immediate requirements, virtually all of them can be oven dried, allowed to cool and then placed in a glass storage jar with an airtight lid. You can if you wish grind them before storing, but on the whole the flavour seems to be best retained by storing them unground and then grinding them only when required.

APPETIZERS

Avocado Savoury

1 avocado
½ cupful mung bean sprouts (oven-dried)
1 dessertspoonful lemon juice or cider
vinegar
slice of lemon

Cut the avocado in half, put a small quantity of lemon juice or cider vinegar in the centre, then place a slice of lemon upright in the middle. Sprinkle oven-dried sprouts around the edge and in the centre but leave the top half of the lemon slice clearly visible.

Pine and Sprout Savoury

2 pineapple rings (fresh or canned)
½ cupful triticale
¼ cupful oven-dried mung sprouts

Put the first pineapple ring on a bed of triticale, cover this with more triticale and place the second ring on top. Garnish with dried mung sprouts.

Soya Lentil Soup

2 oz. (50g) reconstituted mince soya protein
2 cupsful lentil sprouts
3 cupsful water
1 small chopped onion
2 chopped carrots
1 tablespoonful yeast extract
herb salt to taste

Reconstitute the soya protein, put it in water and cook with the onion. Add lentil sprouts, carrots and yeast extract, with herb salt to taste. Cook slowly for 30 minutes.

Sprout Stuffed Tomatoes

4 medium tomatoes
1 teaspoonful alfalfa sprouts
1 dessertspoonful lentil sprouts
1 dessertspoonful sunflower seed sprouts
1 dessertspoonful each: spring onions, celery, red
or green pepper, all chopped
2 hard-boiled eggs, sliced
tomato dressing (see below)

Cut the tops from the tomatoes and scoop out the pulp. Combine the chopped pulp and other ingredients with the dressing. Fill the tomato shells and garnish with more alfalfa sprouts and egg slices.

Tomato Dressing

2 tablespoonful lemon juice
2 tablespoonsful mayonnaise
sea salt and paprika to taste

Super Soup

7 cupsful water
$\frac{1}{2}$ cupful adzuki beans
$\frac{1}{4}$ cupful blackeye beans
1 oz. (25g) adzuki sprouts
1 oz. (25g) mung sprouts
2 carrots
2 onions
1 oz. (25g) water cress
1 oz. (25g) soya flour
$\frac{1}{2}$ teaspoonful sea salt
1 teaspoonful yeast extract
    1 oz. (25g) vegetable margarine or vegetable oil

Soak the beans overnight, slice the onions, dice the carrots, finely chop the sprouts and cress. Bring the water to the boil and leave on a low heat. Add the sea salt and yeast extract, then stir in the soya flour and vegetable margarine (or oil). Add the pre-soaked beans, carrots and onions, stirring continuously, then allow to cook for 40 minutes. Finally, add the sprouts and cress, and cook for a further 10 minutes.

Zesty Baked Eggs in Individual Ramekins

For one person:

1 egg
½ teaspoonful mustard
5 drops soy sauce
¼ cupful lentil bean sprouts, chopped
¼ cupful radish sprouts, chopped
¼ cupful grated cheese

Set oven at Gas No. 4/350°F (180°C). Smear sunflower oil on the inside of the ramekin, break in the egg and stir with fork. Stir in all the other ingredients in the stated order, but allow part of the cheese to cover the other ingredients. Place the ramekins in a *bain-marie* and bake for 20-30 minutes until firm. Serve at once.

SALADS

Cole-slaw

1 small cabbage
1 large sharp apple
1 large carrot
8 oz. (225g) mung bean sprouts
1 onion
2 oz. (50g) pure lemon juice
6 oz. (175g) mayonnaise

Shred the mung bean sprouts very finely. Then shred the cabbage, carrot, apple, and onion, and add the finely shredded bean sprouts. Sprinkle with the lemon juice and then toss in the mayonnaise.

Dandelion and Sprout Side Salad

1 teaspoonful cider vinegar
2 teaspoonful sunflower seed oil
1 oz. (25g) alfalfa sprouts
1 oz. (25g) dandelion leaves
1 lettuce
1 tablespoonful chopped chives

Select the dandelion leaves from tender young plants, wash and separate the lettuce leaves, and toss the dandelion, lettuce and sprouts. Blend sunflower oil and cider vinegar and dress the salad. Toss the salad again and serve.

For added variety and appearance, chopped nuts can be sprinkled on top.

Egg and Tomato Salad

4 hard-boiled eggs
4 large tomatoes
4 tablespoonsful mung bean sprouts
1 lettuce
mayonnaise

Arrange shredded lettuce on a dish and top with 8 slices of tomato. Place half an egg on each and spoon over a little mayonnaise. Place the bean sprouts in the centre and garnish with the remaining tomato slices.

Super Cheese Sprout Salad

2 cupsful lentil sprouts
2 cupsful alfalfa sprouts
2 cupsful mung bean sprouts
$\frac{1}{2}$ cupful wheat sprouts
$\frac{1}{2}$ cupful radish sprouts
$\frac{1}{2}$ cupful sunflower sprouts
grated cheese

Toss all the sprouts together gently and serve topped with the grated cheese.

Winter Vitamin Salad

grated Brussel sprouts
grated parsnip
grated swede
grated raw beetroot
radishes, thinly sliced
olives (optional)
shredded cabbage
celery, chopped
onion, finely chopped
mixed bean sprouts
French dressing

Toss combined vegetables in dressing and serve on bed of green (lettuce, cabbage, and so on). Top with walnuts and slices of red apple.

CHEESE DISHES

Cheese and Sprout Fondue

7 oz. (200g) Emmenthal cheese
3 oz. (75g) dry white wine
1 teaspoonful cornflour
3 oz. (75g) oven dried alfalfa sprouts
paprika and kirsch to taste
pinch of nutmeg

Rub a fondue dish with garlic, slice the cheese and put into the dish with the wine. Add the paprika and nutmeg. When the mixture starts to bubble, add the kirsch, cornflour and dried sprouts. Stir continuously until smooth. Use with wholemeal bread cut into squares.

Macaroni Cheese

4 oz. (100g) wholemeal macaroni
1 oz. (25g) vegetable margarine
4 tablespoonsful cream or top of the milk
4 oz. (100g) grated cheese
1 clove garlic
$\frac{1}{2}$ teaspoonful dry mustard
1 large onion
2 oz. (50g) bean sprouts

Chop and fry the onion with the crushed garlic in a small quantity of sunflower oil, adding the sprouts when the mixture has softened. Put aside. Cook the macaroni in boiling salted water until tender, drain and toss in the melted margarine, cream and cheese. Finally, stir in the onion mixture and serve.

Potato Cheese with Sprouts

1$\frac{1}{2}$ lb (675g) potatoes
2 oz. (50g) butter
top of the milk
8 oz. (225g) (or more if liked) grated cheese
2 oz. (50g) triticale sprouts

Boil the potatoes, drain and mash them with butter, milk and seasoning to a creamy consistency, then beat in the grated cheese. Stir in the triticale sprouts and place in a buttered fireproof dish in a moderate oven until brown and crisp on top – about 20-30 minutes.

MAIN DISHES

Chinese Omelette

2 medium onions
1 oz. (25g) mung bean sprouts
1 oz. (25g) adzuki sprouts
4 oz. (100g) mushrooms
1 clove garlic
1 oz. (25g) unpolished rice
1 tablespoonful sunflower oil
sea salt
2 teaspoonsful soya sauce
½ pt. (275ml) water
4 eggs

Chop the onions, mushrooms and garlic and fry with the rice in the oil for a few minutes. Add the soya sauce, stock and sprouts, season with salt and continue cooking for 10-15 minutes. Make 2 omelettes with the 4 eggs, 4 tabelespoonsful water and seasoning. Fill with the mixture and serve.

Fried Sprouts and Rice

4 cupsful cooked unpolished rice
1 carrot
1 onion
1 oz. (25g) soya sprouts
2 oz. (50g) mung sprouts
1 teaspoonful yeast extract
2 tablespoonsful sunflower oil

Heat the sunflower oil in an open pan. Finely chop the carrot, onion, soya and mung sprouts, mix with the rice and stir gently for 3 minutes. Add the yeast extract and continue to mix for a further 3 minutes. Allow to heat through on low heat for a further 3 minutes and serve.

Frisco Fry

mixed vegetables, including celery, peppers,
   carrot, to taste
7 oz. (200g) cooked unpolished rice
3 tablespoonsful sunflower seed oil
2 dessertspoonsful tamari
2 oz. (50g) adzuki and mung bean sprouts
1 bunch spring onions

Slice the onions and *sauté* in sunflower oil
until transparent, then add the sliced
vegetables and the sprouts and *sauté* for 5
minutes. Add the rice and *sauté* for a
further 5 minutes, stirring frequently.
Finally, add the tamari and sea salt to taste,
and allow to cook for 3 minutes.

Fruit and Sprout Curry

2 medium apples, chopped
$\frac{1}{2}$ cupful celery, sliced
2 cloves garlic
1 tablespoonful ginger root, finely chopped
1 medium onion, chopped
1-1$\frac{1}{2}$ tablespoonsful curry powder
1$\frac{1}{2}$ teaspoonful cinamon
3 tablespoonsful wholemeal flour
3 cupsful soya milk and shredded coconut, or
   coconut milk
1 banana, sliced
$\frac{1}{2}$ cupful alfalfa sprouts
$\frac{1}{2}$ cupful mung bean sprouts
$\frac{1}{4}$ cupful lentil sprouts

Sauté the celery, garlic and onion in a small
amount of sunflower oil, add the apple and
stir for 2 minutes. Add the curry powder,
cinnamon and flour, and cook for 1
minute. Stir in 1 cupful of coconut milk and
simmer until the apple is tender but not

soft. Add the sliced banana, sprouts and ginger root and continue simmering until soft. Pour in the remainder of the coconut milk and correct the seasoning. Serve with steamed brown rice.

Haricot Stew

½ lb (225g) haricot beans
1 large carrot
2 large potatoes
1 medium onion
2 medium leeks
1 stick celery
1 oz. (25g) sunflower oil
herbs to taste
salt to taste
2 cupsful mixed bean sprouts

Soak the beans overnight and cook in the same water next day until soft (40 minutes). Prepare the vegetables and cut into cubes. Cook in the oil until not quite soft. Add to the beans and cook together until all are quite soft. There should be very little water left by now. Mix in the herbs and salt. Heat again and stir in the bean sprouts just before serving.

Macro Meal

2 oz. (50g) unpolished rice
1 tablespoonful miso
½ lb. (225g) mixed adzuki, red wonder and soya
   beans
3 oz. (75g) mixed adzuki, red wonder and soya
   bean sprouts
2 oz. (50g) diced carrots
2 sticks celery, chopped
2 onions, sliced

Soak the beans overnight in 4 times their own volume of water. Put them in a casserole with the rice and vegetables. Dissolve the miso in a small quantity of water and add to the casserole. Cook in a slow oven for about 5 hours, adding more water if necessary. Add the sprouts for the last $\frac{1}{2}$ hour of the cooking time.

Sprout Protein Casserole

1 cupful unpolished rice
1 teaspoonful salt
1 tablespoonful butter
5 oz. (125g) soya protein (plain or beef flavoured)
1 clove garlic, crushed
1 small onion, chopped
1 green pepper, chopped
4 large tomatoes, chopped
basil and oregano to taste
$\frac{1}{2}$ cupful lentil sprouts
$\frac{1}{2}$ cupful mung bean sprouts
$\frac{1}{4}$ cupful radish sprouts
$\frac{3}{4}$ cupful grated cheese

Cook the rice in 2 cupful of boiling water. Add the salt and butter. Reconstitute the soya protein and add to the browned onion, green pepper and garlic. Add the tomatoes, basil and oregano, and simmer until it begins to thicken. Stir in the sprouts. Put layers of rice and the mixture into a casserole and sprinkle with cheese. Bake at Gas No. 4/350°F (180°C) for 20 minutes.

Stuffed Marrow

1 medium-sized marrow
4 oz. (100g) unpolished rice
2 onions
2 oz. (50g) butter
4 oz. (100g) mushrooms, sliced
2 large tomatoes, skinned and chopped
2 tablespoonsful lentil sprouts
seasoning

Cut the marrow in half and spoon out the seeds. Cook the rice in boiling salted water and drain. *Sauté* the chopped onions in butter until soft, add the mushrooms, tomatoes and sprouts, and *sauté* for a further 2-3 minutes. Combine with the cooked rice, season to taste and put the mixture in one half of the marrow. Place the remaining half on top, wrap in foil and bake in a moderate – Gas No. 4/350°F (180°C) – oven until tender – about $\frac{3}{4}$-1 hour. Serve with tomato sauce.

Sprout Pancakes

1 cupful 81% plain flour
$\frac{1}{2}$ cupful mung bean sprouts
1 cupful milk
3 eggs
2 tablespoonsful butter or sunflower oil
seasoning

Put the flour, salt and pepper in a bowl, break eggs into a well in the centre and gradually beat in, using one-third of the milk. Beat for 10 minutes, then stir in the remainder of the milk and leave to stand for 30 minutes. Cook the pancakes in the usual way, placing the bean sprouts in the centre before rolling up.

Stuffed Peppers

4 green peppers
4 oz. (100g) unpolished rice
2 onions
1 clove garlic
2 oz. (50g) ground cashews or brazils
4 tablespoonful tomato *purée*
2 tablespoonful bean sprouts
sunflower oil
seasoning

Cut the top off the peppers and scoop out the seeds. Cook the rice in boiling salted water, and drain. *Sauté* the onions with the crushed garlic in 1 tablespoonful of sunflower oil. When soft, combine with the rice, nuts and sprouts, and mix well, seasoning to taste. Put the mixture into the peppers, pour a dessertspoonful of oil on each pepper and bake in a moderate oven – Gas No. 4/350°F (180°C) – for 40-45 minutes, basting occasionally.

Vegetable and Sprout Pie

Crust:

2½ cupsful wholemeal flour
1 teaspoonful sea salt
¾ cupful sunflower or corn oil
5 tablespoonful water

Put the flour in a bowl and knead in the oil. Add the salt to the water and then add the water to the flour in the bowl, continuing to knead all the time. Finally, roll out and form into a lining for a pie dish, keeping enough pastry to cover the pie.

Filling:

1 oz. (25g) soya flour
3 oz. (75g) water
½ oz. (15g) fenugreek sprouts
1 oz. (25g) mung bean sprouts
1 parsnip
1 carrot
1 onion
1 oz. (25g) yeast extract
1 oz. (25g) sea salt

Finely slice the parsnip and the onion, and dice the carrot. Put the water in a pan and add the salt, yeast extract and soya flour. Blend well together and then add the sprouts and vegetables and cook for 15 minutes, stirring all the time. Place the mixture in the pie and cover with the remaining pastry. Prick top with fork and cook for 35 minutes at Gas No. 4/350°F (180°C).

VEGETABLE DISHES

Croquet Potatoes

1 lb (450g) cooked potatoes
1 oz. (25g) triticale sprouts
seasoning
brown breadcrumbs
1 egg, beaten

Add the sprouts to the mashed potato and mix in the beaten egg. Shape into small rolls and dip in the beaten egg and brown breadcrumbs. Deep fry until golden brown.

Spiced Turnips and Carrots

1 green pepper
2 oz. (50g) fenugreek sprouts
2 small onions
½ teaspoonful turmeric
1 teaspoonful chilli powder
8 oz. (225g) each carrots and turnips
sunflower oil
sea salt

Slice the onions and pepper, and dice the carrot and turnip. Fry the onions and pepper in 1 tablespoonful sunflower oil until soft. Add the turmeric and chilli powder, and mix well. Then add the vegetables and fenugreek sprouts and enough water to prevent burning. Cover and simmer until just soft, adding salt to taste.

BREADS AND CAKES

Malt and Sprout Loaf

8 oz. (225g) wholemeal flour (SR)
2 oz. (50g) finely chopped alfalfa sprouts
¼ pt. (100ml) warm water
2 oz. (50g) molasses
3 oz. (75g) malt extract
1 egg
3 oz. (75g) seedless raisins or sultanas
1 teaspoonful sunflower oil

Mix the flour with the water, molasses, malt extract and sunflower oil in a bowl and leave in a warm place for 45 minutes. Then add the beaten egg, sprouts and chosen fruit. Put in a greased 1 lb (450g) tin and bake for 1-1½ hours in a moderate oven – about Gas No. 4/350°F (180°C).

Nut and Sprout Slice

3½ cupsful plain 81% flour
2 oz. (50g) muscovado sugar
2 oz. (50g) honey
1 teaspoonful sea salt
½ cupful ground cashews
½ cupful chopped hazelnuts
1 cupful finely chopped alfalfa sprouts
2 teaspoonsful baking powder

Mix together the flour, sprouts and ground cashews. Add the baking powder and salt. Stir in the honey, sugar and chopped hazels. Put into a greased baking tin and bake at Gas No. 4/350°F (180°C) for 30-40 minutes. Cut into slices and allow to cool.

Rice/Grain Bread

1 teaspoonful brown sugar
1 tablespoonful finely chopped rice sprouts
1 tablespoonful finely chopped adzuki sprouts
2 cupsful wholewheat flour
½ teaspoonful sea salt
1 tablespoonful soya flour
1 tablespoonful sunflower oil
2 cupsful unpolished rice
1 oz. (25g) fresh yeast
water as required

Grind the rice to a coarse flour and mix with the wholewheat flour and soya flour. Cream the yeast and sugar and add to the rice and flour mixture. Sprinkle salt into the mix and add oil. Pour in water gradually to make a good workable dough. (The water must be added slowly to prevent the mixture getting too wet). Finally, add the chopped sprouts, allow to rise for about half an hour and then knock back and place into tins or mould in cobs.

Leave for 5 minutes, then bake for 35-45 minutes at Gas No. 5/375°F (190°C).

Spice Cake

4 tablespoonsful butter
½ cupful roasted and ground soya sprouts
¾ cupful brown sugar
2 cupsful 81% flour
½ teaspoonful cinnamon
½ teaspoonful nutmeg
2 oz. (50g) molasses
2 eggs
½ cupful milk
2 teaspoonsful baking powder
½ cupful chopped walnuts
½ cupful sultanas or seedless raisins

Mix the flour, baking powder and spices together, rub in the butter, then stir in the sugar. Beat the eggs and milk and add to the dry ingredients, together with the molasses. Finally, stir in the ground sprouts, fruit and walnuts and beat well. Place in prepared cake tin and bake at Gas No. 5/375°F (190°C) for 30-40 minutes.

Sprout Buns

As for rice grain bread but add 2 oz. (50g) vostizza currants 1 oz. (25g) *additional* soya flour, and 1 oz. (25g) sugar. After mixing and allowing to rise, mould into separate buns, put on a baking tray and cook for 25-30 minutes.

Traditional Wholemeal Sprout Bread

3 lbs (1.2kg) wholemeal flour
2 level teaspoonsful muscovado or demerara
    sugar
1½ pt. (850ml) lukewarm water
2 oz. (50g) fresh yeast or 1 oz. (25g) dried yeast
8 oz. (225g) wheat sprouts
1 oz. (25g) sunflower seed oil or vegetable
    margarine
1½ level teaspoonsful salt

Stand the flour in a mixing bowl in a warm place and add the finely chopped sprouts. Dissolve 1 teaspoonful of sugar in ½ pt. (275ml) warm water, then blend in the fresh yeast or mix in the dried yeast with a fork. Leave for approximately 5 minutes. Add oil or margarine to the flour, mixing in well. Dissolve the salt and remaining sugar in the rest of the water and add this with the yeast mixture to the flour. Mix thoroughly to form a good workable dough and knead on a floured board. Cover the dough and leave in a warm place for 30 minutes. Knead again and then divide the dough into four equal parts, placing each in a well-greased 1 lb (450g) baking tin. Cover the tins and leave on one side in a warm place for about quarter of an hour. Bake at Gas No. 8/450°F (230°C) for 35-40 minutes.

DIPS, SAUCES AND SPREADS

Avocado Dip

1 cupful mung sprouts
1 avocado
4 oz. (100g) cream cheese
1 tablespoonful sunflower oil
½ cupful oven-dried lentil sprouts
herb salt

Mash the avocado in a bowl. Add the cream cheese, sunflower oil, herb salt and mung sprouts. Whisk together briskly, add the lentil sprouts and mix thoroughly.

Cheese Dip

1 cupful lentil sprouts
5 oz. (150g) cream cheese
2 tablespoonsful yogurt
¼ cupful finely chopped chives
½ teaspoonful herb salt

Soften the cream cheese and very gradually stir in the yogurt. Whisk briskly, then add the remaining ingredients, giving the mixture a final whisk.

Cheese and Sprout Spread

1 lb (450g) strong Cheddar cheese
4 oz. (100g) cream cheese
4 tablespoonsful sunflower oil
4 tablespoonsful medium sherry
1 teaspoonful dry mustard
1 tablespoonful mixed mung and alfalfa sprouts,
   finely chopped.

Grate the cheese, then mix in the cream cheese, oil, sherry, and mustard, blending well. Finally, stir in the sprouts.

Sesame Seed Sauce for Sprout Salads

¾ cupful sesame seeds
½ cupful corn oil
1½ cupsful water (more or less, according to
    required consistency)
1-3 tablespoonsful soya sauce
½ tablespoonful herb salt
1 tablespoonful brewer's yeast (optional)
2-3 cloves garlic, crushed

Blend all the ingredients until smooth.

Shanghai Savoury Spread

1 oz. (25g) dried and finely ground mung sprouts
1 oz. (25g) dried and finely ground soya sprouts
1 teaspoonful sea salt (fine)
2 oz. (50g) peanut butter (smooth)
1 oz. (25g) vegetable margarine
1 teaspoonful tomato *purée*
½ teaspoonful yeast extract

Blend the peanut butter and vegetable margarine, and add the yeast extract, sea salt, and tomato *purée*. Continue to blend, adding the ground sprouts, and mix well until completely smooth.

Sprout and Bran Breakfast Mix

1 oz. (25g) dried and ground alfalfa sprouts (fresh
    ones could be used)
½ oz. (15g) crushed wheat
1 oz. (25g) rolled oats
½ oz. (15g) millet flakes
½ oz. (15g) milk powder
1 oz. (25g) bran

Mix all the ingredients together thoroughly. Serve with milk and sugar.

Sprout and Miso Spread

1 oz. (25g) 81% flour
½ oz. (15g) fenugreek sprouts
1½ oz. (40g) adzuki bean sprouts
1 tablespoonful miso
1 tablespoonful sunflower oil
1 oz. (25g) peanut butter

Chop the sprouts very finely, ensuring that no husks are left. Heat the oil in a small pan, add the sprouts and flour and stir thoroughly. Stir in the miso and peanut butter for 1 minute. Allow to cool.

Sprout and Tomato Chutney

1½ lb (675g) green tomatoes
4 oz. (100g) fenugreek or triticale sprouts
12 oz. (350g) cooking apples
1½ lb (675g) onions
1 lb (450g) muscovado sugar
1 pt. (575ml) cider apple vinegar
1 dessertspoonful curry powder
1 dessertspoonful turmeric
1 dessertspoonful ground mixed spice

Peel and chop the apples. Chop the tomatoes, put them in a bowl and cover with boiling water for 2 minutes. Simmer all the ingredients together for 30 minutes. Allow to cool and put into jars for storage.

Index